TRUCK
TALK

For those drivers—working by night and day—their eyes on the road—hour after hour, mile after mile. Above the din of the highway and the radio, their ears are always tuned in, alert, ready to listen to a particular voice—truck talk.

—B.K.

TRUCK TALK

Rhymes on Wheels

by Bobbi Katz

SCHOLASTIC INC.

New York London Toronto Auckland Sydney

Photo Credits

Front Cover: Lowell Tindell; **pp. 3, 9** *bottom right,* **30** *first row, middle:* John David Fleck / Gamma-Liaison; **pp. 5, 30** *first row, left:* R. Dahlquist / Superstock; **pp. 6, 30** *second row, right:* Lowell Tindell; **p. 7** *top left:* Lowell Tindell; *top right:* Richard Gross / West Stock; **pp. 8, 30** *second row, left:* Mia & Klaus / Superstock; **p. 9** *bottom left:* Charlie Westerman / Gamma-Liaison; **p. 10:** Larry Mulvehill / The Imageworks; **p. 11** *top left:* Chris Baker / Tony Stone Images; *top right* and **p. 30** *second row, middle:* Ed Pritchard / Tony Stone Images; **p. 12** Lowell Tindell; **p. 13** *bottom left:* Scott Barrow; *bottom right:* Marc St. Gil / West Stock; **p. 14:** Morris Best / Uniphoto; **p. 15:** *top left* and **p. 30** *third row, middle:* Morris Best / Uniphoto; *top right:* K. Moan / Superstock; **p. 16:** Sotographs / Gamma-Liaison; **p. 17** *bottom left:* Sotographs / Gamma-Liaison; *bottom right:* Sotographs / Gamma-Liaison; **pp. 18, 30** *third row, right:* Joseph Sohm / The Image Works; **p. 19** *top left:* Tom Carroll / International Stock; *top right:* Scott Barrow; **p. 20:** Robert Llewellyn / Superstock; **p. 21** *bottom left:* Lester Sloan / Gamma-Liaison; *bottom right* and **p. 30** *first row, right:* K. Moan / Superstock; **p. 22:** Lowell Tindell; **p. 23** *top left:* Margot Granitsas / The Image Works; *top right:* Lowell Tindell; **p. 24:** Dennis Fisher / International Stock; **p. 25** *bottom left:* Lowell Tindell; *bottom right:* Bruce Forster / Tony Stone Images; **pp. 26, 30** *third row, left:* Lowell Tindell; **p. 27** *top left:* Thomas Wanstall / The Image Works; *top right:* Paul Kotz / West Stock; **p. 28:** Lowell Tindell; **p. 29** *bottom left:* Lowell Tindell; *bottom right:* Lowell Tindell; **p. 32:** Lowell Tindell; **Back Cover:** Lowell Tindell.

Digital retouching by Karin Aberg for pp. **8, 10, 12, 13** *bottom left,* **13** *bottom right,* **16, 17** *bottom right,* **18, 22, 24, 26, 28, front cover** and **back cover.**

Library of Congress Cataloging-in-Publication Data

Katz, Bobbi.
    Truck talk / by Bobbi Katz.
        p.   cm.
    "Cartwheel books."
    Summary: A collection of poems in which various kinds of trucks, including a garbage truck, a tow truck, a cement mixer, and a fire truck, describe what they do.
    ISBN 0-590-69328-X
    1. Truck—Juvenile poetry.   2. Children's poetry, American.
    [1. Trucks—Poetry.   2. American poetry.]   I. Title.
    PS3561.A7518T78   1997
    811'.54—dc20

                                                                96-21306
                                                                CIP
                                                                AC

12 11 10 9 8 7 6 5 4 3 2 1   7 8 9/9 0 1 2/0
                        Printed in Singapore   46

First Scholastic printing, April 1997

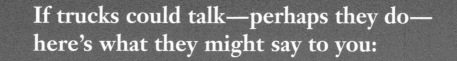

**If trucks could talk—perhaps they do—
here's what they might say to you:**

Ambulance

Someone needs me. Someone's sick.
Hurry! Hurry!
Quick! Quick! Quick!
My siren howls a warning cry:
Cars and people, let me by!
Medics ride along with me,
expecting an emergency.
We're prepared to act with speed
to get folks all the care they need.

Trailer Truck

We are buddies. What a pair!
We go together everywhere.
What's a cab without a trailer?
Like a ship without a sailor!

We whiz along the interstate.
From coast to coast, we carry freight.
Oh, how wonderful it feels
to roll along on eighteen wheels!

Tow Truck

When I know there's a car to tow,
I flash my lights and off I go!
Mud and snow and slippery ice
give my work some added spice.
I'll hook my hook right to your car
and pull you out of where you are.
And if your car needs extra care,
choose a garage. I'll tow you there!

Car Transport Truck

New cars, new cars, take a ride.
Let me show you the countryside!
Red, tan, yellow—
　　　　　green, gray, blue—
I'll gladly carry *all* of you.
Climb upon my metal track,
and you can travel piggyback!

Moving Truck

Look for me on moving day.
I'll come and cart your stuff away.
Nothing is too large or small.
I have room to take it all!
Wrapped and strapped, each piece will fit.
I'll take good care of every bit.
At your new house you will see,
that you were right to count on me.

Delivery Truck

I am slick and slim and tailored
to slip neatly through the streets.
I am happy to deliver
fresh-cut flowers, toys, or treats.
My side panels tell my story—
where I work and what I do.
My back door can unlock quickly.
I might bring a bike to you!

Cement Mixer

What do I get fed for breakfast?
Water, gravel, and some sand!
Next it's up to me to mix it.
Take a look. You'll understand.
You can see my belly turning,
churning 'round and 'round and 'round.
When I get where I am going,
I drop gray glop to the ground.
Busy guys in black galoshes
spread and smooth it while it's wet.
Cement soup that I deliver
turns to sidewalk when it's set.

Fire Trucks

Fire! Fire! Brnng! Brnng! BRNNG!
Into action we both spring.
Sirens shrieking, metal gleaming,
down the streets we both go streaming.
We're a team and, two by two,
we do the job we're meant to do.
Pumper's hoses will deliver
water to make hot flames shiver.
Hook and Ladder brings the crew
to high floors where there's work to do.

Ice Cream Truck

"Jingle-jangle-jingle-jangle..."
When you hear me sing my song,
you will know that summer's coming
and, of course, you won't be wrong.
I'm the knight in bright white armor.
Choose a sweet and icy treat!
Winter winds still blow inside me,
as I help you beat the heat.

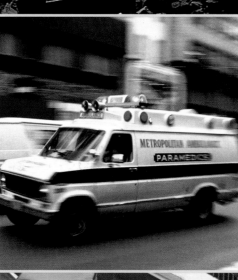

So many different kinds of trucks
help people every day.
And *now* when one goes rolling by,
you'll know what it might say!